Scotland's
MALT
WHISKIES

A Dram by Dram Guide

by John Wilson

Illustrations: Elizabeth Lyon

First published 1973 by Famedram Publishers Gartocharn Scotland UK
Reprinted and copyright 1974, 1975, 1976, 1977, 1978

The Distilleries

ABERLOUR-GLENLIVET	Aberlour, Banffshire
ARDBEG	Isle of Islay
✓ AUCHENTOSHAN	Old Kilpatrick, Dumbartonshire
AULTMORE	Keith, Banffshire
BALBLAIR	Edderton, Tain, Ross-shire
BALVENIE	Dufftown, Banffshire
BLADNOCH	Wigtown, Wigtownshire
BLAIR ATHOL	Pitlochry, Perthshire
BOWMORE	Isle of Islay
BRUICHLADDICH	Isle of Islay
CAPERDONICH	Rothes, Morayshire
CARDHU	Knockando, Morayshire
CLYNELISH	Brora, Sutherland
DALMORE	Dalmore, Ross-shire
DEANSTON MILL	Doune, Perthshire
DUFFTOWN-GLENLIVET	Dufftown, Banffshire
GLENDEVERON (MacDuff)	Banff, Banffshire
GLENDRONACH	Huntly Aberdeenshire
GLENDULLAN	Dufftown, Banffshire
GLENFARCLAS-GLENLIVET	Ballindalloch, Banffshire
✓ GLENFIDDICH	Dufftown, Banffshire
GLEN FLAGLER (Moffat)	Airdrie, Lanarkshire
GLEN GARIOCH	Oldmeldrum, Aberdeenshire
GLENGOYNE	Dumgoyne, Stirlingshire
GLEN GRANT-GLENLIVET	Rothes, Morayshire
✓ THE GLENLIVET	Glenlivet, Banffshire
GLEN MHOR	Inverness, Inverness-shire
GLENMORANGIE	Tain, Ross-shire
GLENROTHES-GLENLIVET	Rothes, Morayshire
GLEN SCOTIA	Campbeltown, Argyllshire
✓ GLENTURRET	Crieff, Perthshire
HIGHLAND PARK	Kirkwall, Isle of Orkney
INCHGOWER	Buckie, Banffshire
JURA	Isle of Jura, Argyllshire
KNOCKANDO	Knockando, Morayshire

✓ Drumguish   Drumguish, Inverness-shire
(med-dark, peaty-smokey)
GLEN MORAY   Elgin, Morayshire
(smooth taste - not smoky)

LAGAVULIN	Isle of Islay
LAPHROAIG	Isle of Islay
LINKWOOD	Elgin, Morayshire
LITTLEMILL	Bowling, Dunbartonshire
LONGMORN-GLENLIVET	Longmorn, Elgin, Morayshire
MACALLAN	Craigellachie, Banffshire
MILTONDUFF-GLENLIVET	Elgin, Morayshire
MORTLACH-GLENLIVET	Dufftown, Banffshire
OBAN	Oban, Argyllshire
OLD FETTERCAIRN	Fettercairn, Kincardineshire
OLD PULTENEY	Wick, Caithness
ORD	Muir of Ord, Ross-shire
ROSEBANK	Falkirk, Stirlingshire
SPRINGBANK	Campbeltown, Argyllshire
STRATHISLA-GLENLIVET	Keith, Banffshire
TALISKER	Carbost, Isle of Skye
TAMDHU-GLENLIVET	Knockando, Morayshire
TAMNAVULIN-GLENLIVET	Ballindalloch, Banffshire
TOMATIN	Tomating, Inverness-shire
TOMINTOUL-GLENLIVET	Ballindalloch, Banffshire
TORMORE	Advie, Grantown-on-Spey, Morayshire
TULLIBARDINE	Blackford, Perthshire

✓ McCLELLAND's (ISLAY)   T. A. McClelland LTd, Glasgow
(dark, very smoky - strong after taste)

~~Old Fettercairn~~
✓ SPEYBURN   Rothes, Scot.
(smoky, peaty taste)

For details of distilleries that welcome visits from the public
and the times they are open see 'Scotland's Distilleries: A
Visitors' Guide' also by John Wilson. Famedram Publishers.

Introduction

PURE malt whisky is the true and ancient whisky of Scotland. It is nowadays distilled in the same type of pot still and by the same methods as were once operating, often illegally, all over the country. There are only two big differences between then and now. The first is the obvious one of scale and the second is the more important one of maturity.

Whereas once it was drunk straight from the barrel, with all its toxic elements still

present, now malt whisky is matured for years in casks while millions of gallons float away by evaporation into the pure Scottish ether. The legal minimum for maturing is three years but almost all bottled malt whisky sold in this country is matured much longer and right up to 12 years it gains in blandness and smoothness. After that, and some malt whisky is sold much older, the gain in quality is not so pronounced.

Malt whisky is a liqueur, comparable with the finest brandy and to many people is best drunk neat, although at certain times of day just a little water might be wisely added. It is also one of the most interesting spirits in the world, partly because only in Scotland are the climate, water and peat suitable for making it and partly because there is as much variation between each famous name of single malt whisky (that is whisky from one distillery only) as between Château bottled wines of France.

This is true for mysterious reasons which no one has yet been able to analyse. Even where one distillery is only a few hundred yards from another and where the same water and the same size and shape of still is used, subtle differences of taste can always be discerned.

Quite how the art of distilling ever came to Scotland, no one knows although, in the absence of evidence, learned men have had a field day in speculation. Quite possibly the

Introduction: What is malt whisky?

art of distilling was first discovered in
antiquity by the Chinese, brought by Arab
traders to the Middle East and from there was
taken by the Crusaders to Europe, notably to
France and Ireland. It was certainly used for
making perfume and later, by the monasteries
for making all kinds of medicines and herbal
potions. But it was not long before they
discovered that barley lends itself as well as
the grape to the distilling of life-enhancing
spirit and so high was the regard of the monks
for these fiery distillations that they were
called Aqua Vitae or 'water of life.' The
exact translation of this in Gaelic is 'Uisge

Beatha' and the word 'uisge' was later corrupted into the word we know so well.

It is very likely that some of the early monks or Celts brought their expertise in distilling, and even their stills, to the Mull of Kintyre from where the art spread to every

Introduction: What is malt whisky?

part of Scotland. The earliest recorded reference to distilling is in the Scottish Exchequer Rolls of 1494, which describes the provision of 'eight bolls of malt to Friar Cor wherewith to make aquavitae' but it is almost certain that long before that the small crofter's still was everywhere in Scotland.

To make malt whisky, only three ingredients are required and all of them are, in Scotland, in easy supply. They are barley, water and yeast. A grain of barley is a small store of starch and if it can be made to germinate with water and heat, the embryo plant will convert this starch into the sugary maltose.

If barley is first of all steeped in water and then spread on a floor, it will begin to sprout small rootlets. The incipient plant will, after between 10 and 12 days, be ready to call on its reserves of converted starch. At this point it must be stopped, which is done by drying over a fire.

Peat was always the most accessible fuel in Scotland and the smoky, slightly aromatic flavour which it imparts can be tasted in the whisky.

Lately, a taste has developed among many people for a slightly less peated whisky and so coal and anthracite are often used as well. It is this kiln drying of the malt which gives distilleries, with their need for draught, the pagoda-like roofs which, to many people, are their most distinguishing feature. The dried, malted barley is then milled into grist, husks and all, but with the rootlets discarded, to be used as a cattle food. The grist is then subjected to successive, and ever hotter infusions of water, each one taking with it some of the malt until barely any sugar remains.

The liquor is then conducted to great vats, where yeast is added and the fermentation begins. After about 30 hours, the alcohol produced by the action of the yeast inhibits the yeast and the fermentation is almost complete, although small fermentations appear around the edges of liquid. These can be caused by acid-loving microbes or by wild airborne yeasts and to these secondary fermentations credit is often given for some of the attractive character-istics of malt whiskies.

The fermented liquor is then pumped into a receiving vessel in the stillhouse

Introduction: What is malt whisky?

where there are two and sometimes three
great copper stills. The final separation of
the pure spirit begins. The first still is
heated and, as the vapour rises, it passes
through an arm in the neck of the still and
then through a 'worm', a twisting pipe outside
the stillhouse which passes through cold
water. The vapour condenses.

The spirit which comes from the first
still is weak and impure and has to be redis-
tilled in the second still. The gradual
purification of the spirit can be watched in a
glass, brassbound spirit safe where it can be
tested, without human contact, by the addition
of water. If it turns blue, as it does in the
beginning and at the end of every distillation
from the second still, fusil oils are still
present and the liquor must be diverted back
for redistilling. But clear and pure comes the
so called 'middlecut' and this is led away,
reduced from 20 degrees to 11.2 degrees
overproof and then put in sherry or oak casks
to mature. Every stage of the distilling
process, from fermentation on, is watched
and checked by the lynx eyed men of the
Customs and Excise.

The art of distilling malt whisky,
sophisticated as it is in modern practice, is

in essence remarkably simple. Take a sack
of barley and steep it in pure mountain water;
lay out the contents for germination, dry it
over a peat fire, mill it to grist, put it in, say,
a forty gallon tin container with a hole for
drainage and a few sprigs of heather in the
bottom; pour infusions of hot water through
it and collect up the liquor in one of your
available casks; ferment this liquor with
yeast; bung up the bottom of your tin vessel,
pour in the contents of the cask and apply
fire, making sure that an arm leading from the
top of the still is in place and that the 'worm'
from it leads through cold water. Then wait
for the spirit to come forth. Drink it. But
beware. Not only are you doing something
illegal but you will experience bizarre
physical sensations. Bear in mind the
English officers who, in the eighteenth
century tried a trial of strength with just
such raw spirit against a party of Highlanders.
One got incurable gout, one caught a fever,
and the hair of the third fell out. (For those
rash and hazardous people who want to try
such sensations, Messrs Teachers have provided an illustrated booklet.)

Nevertheless, stills very similar to that
described, flourished all over Scotland into
the nineteenth century, from the Highlands

and Islands to the Campsie Fells, in caves
and under canopies of peat and heather.
Even Balfron close to Glasgow was described
by a visitor to Park Hall between 1813 and
1817 as 'a most lawless village.... it was
distillation that demoralised the district. The
men of the place resorted to the woods or
sequestered glens among the Campsie Hills
and there distilled whisky, which their wives
and daughters took in tin vessels in the form
of stays buckled round their waists to sell
for a high price in Glasgow'.

There was little to help the excise officer in the performance of his duties. The terrain was as bad for detection as it could be and the inhabitants hostile to the point of violence. Fire, which is needed at almost every stage of distilling was a help but it was often ingeniously concealed.

One still was finally entered by parting a clump of brambles, lifting a clod of earth, opening a trapdoor which led into a complete underground distillery from which the smoke was led away to join up at a considerable distance with a cottage chimney. Always, the equipment was portable and cheap. Only the copper 'worm', through which the distillate

condensed, was expensive but it was not un-
common for the illicit distiller, to lead the
officers of the law to his outworn plant and
claim the £5 reward for discovering a still.

Private distilling was regarded as a God-
given right and it was often the only means of
livelihood and of paying the rent. But the
Government in London was determined to
check it, to bring it under legal control, and
to mulct it for the benefit of the Treasury.
From the setting up of the Board of Excise
in 1707, successive acts of quite astonishing
ineptitude were passed.

They are best judged by their effects.
The effect of the first tax was to ensure that
the spirit from the illicit stills was better
than that of its legal counterpart. The next
stimulated the distillers to increase their output with such equipment as they had. The
next bore down on the Lowland distillers, to

the benefit of the Highland smugglers. Even
the roads built by General Wade after the '45,
although they made it easier to patrol the
north, never looked like defeating innumerable
smugglers.

Only when, in 1823, reason at last pre-
vailed in the august form of the fifth Duke of
Gordon, did the tide finally turn against the
smuggler. (The word 'smuggler' is used to
describe both the distiller and the transporter
of illicit whisky.) The noble Duke, who was
a great landowner in Inverness-shire and
Banffshire, argued in the house of Lords that
you could not stop the Highlander from distilling, but that if realistic and reasonably
favourable opportunities could be provided
for manufacturing whisky legally, he and his
fellow landowners in Scotland would do their
best to suppress illicit distilling in Scotland
and would encourage their tenants to take out
licences for their stills.

In 1823, an Act was passed which
sanctioned the distilling of whisky on pay-
ment of duty of 2/3d per gallon of proof
spirit and a licence fee of £10 on all stills
with a capacity of 40 gallons or over. The
effect of this act was by no means immediate
but it was progressive. 14,000 stills were

detected in 1823, 692 in 1834, 73 in 1854, 19 in 1864 and 6 in 1874.

In 1833 came one of the epoch-making events in the history of whisky. A retired Inspector of the Customs and Excise in Ireland, one Aeneas Coffey, invented a still capable of producing whisky in great volume from a mixture of malted barley, unmalted rye and maize. One grain whisky distillery can, in fact, make as much grain whisky in a week by a process of continous distillation as a malt distillery produces in a whole season of 40 weeks.

At once there was uproar among the malt distillers, who brought a court case to prevent this rather tasteless spirit from calling itself 'Scotch Whisky'. They lost their case and some years later the firm John Dewar and Sons found grain whisky its true role by using it to make blended whisky, with its appeal for those more fragile, or at least less excercised constitutions which had difficulty in coping with the more potent pure malt whiskies. Blended whisky, helped by the plague of phylloxera which ravaged the vines of France towards the end of the nineteenth century and destroyed the supplies of cognac, began its progress to all parts of the world.

So great was its success that the inevitable
overproduction followed and, in 1898, the
bonanza firm of Pattison's crashed, sending
tremors through the whole whisky industry
and forcing many distilleries to close.

But this short guide is not about
blended whiskies, indeed with close on 3000
of them on the market it would be a curious
document if it were. Nor is it about the vatted
(mixed) malts such as Highland Fusilier,
Findlater's Mar Lodge, Glencoe, Glenleven,
Hudson's Bay 1670, Old Bannockburn, Pride
of Strathspey and Seven Star Special, each of
which has its own distinction and offers a
fine introduction to malt whisky.

It is about those pure single malts which
can be found in bottle. These can be bought
from one of the specialist stockists such as
Gordon and MacPhail of Elgin, Strachan of
Aboyne, Charles Muirhead of Edinburgh or, of
course, Harrods of London. There are many
more licensed grocers in the larger Scottish
towns who are making a feature of single malts:
Fort William, for instance, has several. There
is also a growing number of bars which stock
the full range of available malts.

Introduction: What is malt whisky?

Possibly the most comprehensive collection of whisky bottles on general display — including almost all the malt whiskies — is to be found in 'The Whisky Room' at Cameron House near Balloch. Those who visit the Loch Lomond Bear Park should take the opportunity to see it.

But there is a special pleasure to be had from hunting malt whiskies down in their lairs — or in visiting the distilleries themselves. A visitors' guide to Scotland's distilleries, listing those that do and those that do not welcome visitors, and giving a wealth of handy information, is available as a companion to this guide, from the same publishers.

The traditional classifications of malt whisky are Highland malt, that which comes north of an imaginary line from Greenock to Dundee; Lowland malt, from south of that line; and Islay and Campbeltown malts. But within each area every pure single malt reflects its own country, water, peat, air and history.

If anyone were to want yet another incentive for experimenting the words of James Hogg (1770 — 1830) might serve as a starting point: "If a body could find out the exac' proper proportion and quantity that ought to be drunk and keep to that, I verily trow that he might leeve forever and never die at a', and that doctors and kirkyards would go oot o' fashion.''

He was talking about pure malt whisky, Uisge Beatha, the Water of Life.

JOHN WILSON.

Aberlour-Glenlivet

ABERLOUR-GLENLIVET has associations
with both saints and sinners. The early Christian
missionary St Drostan. baptised his converts in
the waters of Lour before taking up administrative
duties as Abbot of Glastonbury and Archbishop of
Canterbury — leaving the waters for James an
Tuam to convert into quite a different and much
less holy spirit.

James of the Hill, to give him his title in
English, had his cave high on the eastern shoulder
of Benrinnes, near the pool from which the water
cascades 30 feet down the Lynn of Ruthrie to the
site of the present day distillery.

Before the distillery was built this water
provided power to a meal mill and a saw mill.
The early distillery building, built in 1879, was
destroyed by fire and rebuilt after a change of
ownership in 1892.

Since then it has been greatly enlarged, so
much so that capacity has trebled in the last 20
years. But the landscape and trees provide such
cover it is quite easy to pass by without noticing
a distillery exists.

Anyone who climbs the 2765 feet of
Benrinnes, from which (given the statutory clear
day) no fewer that 10 counties are visible, should

be accompanied by an ample dram of the Aberlour-
Glenlivet, bottled at nine years old and 70
degrees of proof.

Ardbeg

ARDBEG is distilled on the south east coast of Islay in a lonely spot on the very edge of the sea.

Before 1815, when the distillery was established, it was the haunt of a notorious band of smugglers who had long been hunted by the authorities. When their hideout was eventually discovered it was feared the smugglers were too strong for open attack.

The excise men had to seize their chance when the gang was away with a boatload of whisky. They appropriated a large amount of the illicit spirit and then destroyed the place.

Thoroughly demoralised, the band broke up and most of its members migrated to the main-land of Kintyre.

Soon after, the founders of the Ardbeg distillery moved into the vacant site to make legitimate use of the exceptionally soft and pure

waters from Loch Arinambeast and Uigeadale. The local peat, which is cut between May and August, is free from offensive materials and very good for drying the malt.

And though the sea around this coast is studded with dangerous rocks, there is a safe anchorage nearby for the supply of the distillery.

Ardbeg whisky, said to be at its best when around eight years old, is by no means easy to come by. There is a small bottling for directors and shareholders and a few cases sometimes find their way into hotels on the island. Unlucky visitors may find that a small investment in the distillery is the only way to secure a bottle!

Auchentoshan

THERE IS an imaginary line drawn from Dundee to Greenock which divides the Highland from the Lowland malts. Auchentoshan is a Lowland malt because the distillery is just south of this line.

Very little peat is used in the firing of the malt. It gives the whisky only the slightest taste. And unlike most of the Highland Malt whiskies which are distilled twice in two pot stills, Auchentoshan is distilled three times in three separate stills.

The first distillation takes an hour, the second five hours, and the third nine hours, until finally the alcohol is separated from all undesirable elements and emerges at 40 degrees over proof. It is then reduced by the addition of soft natural water to 111 degrees and put into oak casks to mature.

If kept for ten years, it is reckoned to lose about 25 per cent of its volume.

Auchentoshan pure malt whisky can be obtained at five years old and 70 degrees of proof from Eadie Cairns, the owners who have an off licence at 91 Hope Street, Glasgow.

The distillery stands hard by the Erskine Bridge, overlooking the Clyde.

Aultmore

AULTMORE was for a long time known as Aultmore-Glenlivet. These were the days when geography was defied in order to gain some of the magic of the Glenlivet name. In fact it was really too far from the famous glen and river and now Aultmore stands in bold isolation.

The distillery itself is somewhat isolated. It is almost the only building that the traveller will see on the road from Keith to Elgin near to the junction

to Buckie. It was built in 1895 by Alexander Edward of Sanquhar Forres and the first distillation came from its stills the following year.

Its position was ordained by the flow of water from the clear springs up in the hills to the north. In 1930 Aultmore came into the possession of John and Robert Harvey and Company Limited. They were subsequently to lease it from the Distillers Company.

Although Aultmore is not heavily promoted it is still sold throughout the world and in fairly small quantities in England and Scotland. Its appeal is specially to those who like their whisky at fullest maturity — 12 years old and 70 proof.

Balblair

BALBAIR malt whisky is distilled within a quarter of a mile of the Dornoch Firth, in an area which once abounded with smuggling bothies.

The distillery, founded in 1749, has claims to being the second oldest in Scotland. It is hardly surprising that distilling has been carried on there for so long because all the local streams are suitable, and the peat, which is used for firing the malt, is both abundant — the whole area is known as the 'parish of peats' — and of a rather special quality.

Probably because of the nature of the peat the peat-flavour is slight and delicate, but the whisky is very aromatic.

Balvenie

BALVENIE is a more recent arrival on the malt whisky scene. Only in 1971 was it widely available as a bottled pure malt — and then in the triangular bottle which had already become familiar through its sister distillery, Glenfiddich.

It was an old Catholic priest that tipped off the original William Grant to the remarkable properties of the Robbie Dubh (pronounced Doo) Spring and when, with the aid of his family, he had built Glenfiddich there he turned his energies to Balvenie.

This distillery takes its name from the ancient castle nearby where once King Edward I ('The Hammer of the Scots') and later, in 1522, Mary, Queen of Scots had stayed.

In 1892 Balvenie Distillery was erected on part of the land purchased for Glenfiddich. It is bottled at 8 years old and 70 degrees of proof.

Bladnoch

BLADNOCH is a Lowland malt and the
distillery is the most southerly of all Scotland's
distilleries. It is only a mile out of Wigton on the
banks of the river Bladnoch. It draws on the waters
of the river Bladnoch which pour down
from the Carrick mountains and are collected in a
dam.

The site of the distillery has now been
enlarged to cover about eight acres and it is
capable of storing 18,000 casks or 1,000,000
proof gallons of Bladnoch malt whisky. The
excise duty on this alone would come to over
£13m.

Bladnoch is a romantic place. On the high
ground above Wigtown is the Martyr's Monument,
commemorating the Covenanters. Near the distillery
is Baldoon farm, where stand the crumbling ruins
of the ancient castle to which Janet Dalrymple,
the 'Bride of Lammermoor', came to die after her
marriage to David Dunbar of Baldoon.

After the depression years of the 1930's,
Bladnoch distillery, which had been famous for
the superb bouquet of its pure malt whisky, was
forced to close, and it was only re-opened in 1956.
But anyone travelling in Galloway today should not
leave without sampling it.

Blair Athol

BLAIR ATHOL, this most distinguished malt whisky, has been distilled in the Vale of Atholl since 1826, when the distillery was built by a Mr Connacher. Mr Connacher was said to have been one of the descendants of the chivalrous young Conacher, an early admirer and companion of the Fair Maid of Perth.

The water for Blair Athol whisky comes direct from Ben Vrachie. It is pure, sparkling and clear as crystal, and was famous for making

whisky long before the establishment of any legal distillery. It was most probably whisky from the caverns of Ben Vrachie which put fire into the Highlanders at the Battle of Killiecrankie, and enabled them to rout the Southerners from the pass.

This attractive distillery, which is now owned by Arthur Bell and Sons, sets out to make visitors welcome*, and since it is located in one of the most beautiful parts of Scotland, it is worth any traveller's while to make a short diversion, especially so because parts of the building are over 200 years old.

They are known to have seen the passage of the Jacobite armies in the 1745 rebellion and to have harboured a fugitive after the rebellion was over.

an early admirer
of the fair Maid of
Perth.'

* For details of times, etc. see 'Scotland's Distilleries: A Visitors' Guide' from the same publishers.

Bowmore

BOWMORE has the distinction of being not only the oldest legal distillery in the island of Islay (it was founded in 1779), but the only one which was actually owned by its occupants. The others were leased from their respective proprietors.

The distillery is especially associated in fairly early days with a family of German origin known as the Mutters. They seem to have prospered greatly during their period of ownership. A James Mutter Senior bore the sonorous title of 'Ottoman, Portuguese and Brazilian Vice-Consul.'

By 1886 there was even a steam vessel, the S.S. James Mutter to be seen near the

the S.S. JAMES MUTTER

distillery. Today the harbour at Bowmore, so long used by the distillery, has finally become silted up with tidal wash and no longer provides a safe anchorage.

The Mutters, who sold the distillery around the turn of the century and went to live in Canada,

started a tradition of technical innovation which
has remained with Bowmore ever since. It had, for
instance, the first condensers of their type and the
first steam-heated stills on the island. In the late
nineteenth century a visitor was surprised to see
there a remarkable still with a 'double-head and
two worms,' a description bound to strike wonder
into the uninitiated.

Bowmore Distillery itself is on the shores
of Loch Indaal, its very walls being lapped by
the sea. It has been suggested that this exposure
to the fresh sea breezes favours all the processes
of distilling while inhibiting harmful bacteria and
fungi. Certainly there are those who even claim
to taste the sea in this fine, subtle Islay malt.

Those who even
claim to taste
the sea....

Bruichladdich

BRUICHLADDICH is a typical Islay malt whisky with a fine flavour. But it lacks that curious 'medicinal' overtone which some people like and others dislike about Laphroaig.

The distillery, which was sited on the sea near Port Charlotte, went out of production during the bad times. In 1960 it was completely modernised and passed into the ownership of Invergordon Distillers Limited.

You will not find here the pagoda roofs which surmount the drying kilns of Bowmore, Ardbeg and Laphroaig across the waters of Loch Indaal where they not only malt their own barley, but hand cut their own peat. Bruichladdich, in common with many of the newer and restored distilleries, prefers to buy in its barley ready malted to its own formula.

Bruichladdich is sold at five years old and 75 degrees of proof, the product of the most westerly of all Scotland's malt whisky distilleries. Go due west of Bruichladdich and you will not encounter another still until you reach the New World.

Caperdonich

CAPERDONICH, the sister distillery to Glen Grant, was originally built in 1897. At that time the excise authorities insisted that the whisky from the new distillery be pumped to Glen Grant

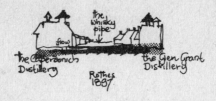

distillery where they were mixed. The 'whisky pipe' crosses the main street of Rothes.

In 1898, the huge and burgeoning whisky blending firm of Pattison crashed with disastrous effects on the distilling industry. Caperdonich was closed in 1901 and did not re-open until 1965.

It is now one of the most modern of all distilleries, almost every operation being controlled by buttons pressed on a central panel.

Caperdonich is only now mature and ready for drinking. To see the subtle difference between the whiskies of two adjacent distilleries, it should be drunk alongside a glass of Glen Grant of comparable age. That is, of course, if you can get it. Such small quantities of Caperdonich have been reaching the home market that this has become one of the rarest among bottled malt whiskies. Serious collectors may prefer to keep their bottle untouched.

Cardhu

CARDHU, which means black rock, is a Speyside whisky, but not a Glenlivet.

The distillery was built in 1824 on the farm of Cardow, where illicit distilling had been carried on for a long time before. Up until about 1890 the distillery had a lease which expired at the end of every 19 years.

The result was a very primitive distillery indeed, where everything was done by hand. The casks of whisky were taken by horse and cart to Burghead in Morayshire and then shipped to Leith.

Now Cardhu, which is owned by Johnny Walker's, is more generally available in the bottle at 12 years of age and 70 degrees of proof. It is reckoned by connoisseurs to go outstandingly well with haggis.

Clynelish

CLYNELISH was born of the Highland Clearances. The distillery was built in 1819 to provide an outlet for the grain produced by those evicted farmers from the interior who had settled on newly cultivated land by the coast.

Its location about a mile from Brora was chosen because of the proximity of the Brora coalfield, coal being needed for power. In actual fact this proved to be of little advantage because although this was the oldest coal mine in Scotland, dating from 1529, its coal was the youngest, at a mere 125 million years old — less than half the usual age, and therefore not of the best quality. From early times the distillery made little use of it.

Clynelish is the most fully flavoured malt whisky outside of Islay and it has a suggestion of ancient sea-weed in its peat mosses. It was a favourite whisky of the great Victorian connoisseur, Prof. Saintsbury.

It can be obtained at various degrees of proof, and a visit to either the Marine Hotel or the Sutherland Arms Hotel in Brora will yield bottles of high strength and many years of maturity.

Dalmore

DALMORE has a superb site on the Cromarty
Firth overlooking the Black Isle. It was founded
in 1839 and to this day has sole rights to the
waters of the river Alness. It also has its own
rail siding and a pier for communication by sea.
Behind, is a high terrace which was in the old
days a rallying point for the Highlanders of the
north against their enemies.

In the First World War it was taken over
by the Admiralty on behalf of the US Navy
as a base for the manufacture of deep sea mines.
During that occupation a large part of the
distillery was burned down and production was
only resumed in 1922. Now, although two stills
dating from 1874 are in continuous use, it is
regarded as one of the finest examples of
modernisation.

Dalmore whisky has its own pier
and railway siding.
R. Alness

The soft and mossy water for Dalmore malt
whisky flows down from the beautiful Loch of
Gildermory, close to Ben Wyvis, over the natural
filter of a gravel bed. It is a quick-maturing
whisky with only a slightly peaty flavour, not
unlike Cardhu.

Deanston Mill

DEANSTON MILL is within a few yards of
commanding one of the more romantic views in
Scotland. But for a frond of trees on the far bank
of the River Teith it would look directly down-
stream to the ruined castle of Doune only a few
bowshots away. The castle appears in a sad
lament for the young 'Bonny Earl of Moray' who
was brutally murdered by the Earl of Huntly at
Donibristle in 1592:

> 'Oh, lang will his lady
> Look owre the Castle Doune
> Ere she sees the Earl of Moray
> Cum soundin' through the towne.'

The qualities which led to the selection of
this site for the building of a cotton mill in 1785,
namely a fine supply of pure, soft water drawn from
high up in the Trossachs, made it possible at a
later date to convert the buildings into a distillery.

Deanston Mill is described by its makers as
having a 'spirit of hidden vigour and an elegant
palate.' At first it could only be bought at the
Blair Drummond safari park, thoughtfully provided
no doubt for the parents of children with strong
desires to get out of the car and stroke the lions.
Now it is to be found at other places too.

Dufftown~Glenlivet

DUFFTOWN is the capital of Scottish malt whisky distilling, as witness the popular couplet —
"Rome was built on seven hills,
Dufftown stands on seven stills."

The Dufftown-Glenlivet distillery is situated in the beautiful Dullan glen, through which the Dullan water flows, 'bright with the snows of Benrinnes'. The water actually used in the whisky comes from Jock's Well, which is famous in the district for its abundant supply of perfect water for distilling.

It is a fine example of a Speyside whisky, bottled at 8 years old and 70 degrees of proof.

Glendeveron

GLENDEVERON is one of the few malt whiskies to take its name from a nearby river instead of the place where it is distilled. The river Deveron, famous for fishing, provides water for this whisky which is distilled in the Macduff Distillery.

Macduff is one of the newer distilleries having been built only in 1960, after a local business man called the attention of Brodie Hepburn Ltd. to the fine local conditions, and the quality of the water to be drawn from a nearby spring.

Glendeveron is bottled as a pure single malt, at 8 years and either at 40 or 43 degrees proof, depending on the market, by Block, Grey and Block of London. It is very lightly peated and popular with the Italians, whose special taste for malt whisky it seems to suit.

Glendronach

GLENDRONACH malt whisky was for a great many years very hard to come by. But since Teacher's took over the distillery in 1960 and enlarged and extended it in 1967 the situation has improved a lot.

It was built in 1826 in a large rookery which was always said to bring luck to distilleries — a relic perhaps of the days when rooks would warn of the approach of the excise officers.

The water for Glendronach comes from the Dronach burn, which runs through the valley of the Forgue, over rich beds of peat and mossy uplands. It is tinged with a golden brown, but very bright and clear, and has a great reputation in the area.

Although by far the larger part of Glendronach's bottled malt whisky goes to export, some can be bought at 8 years old and 80 degrees of proof on the home market.

Glendullan

GLENDULLAN must be the most elusive of all Scotland's single malt whiskies. Apart from the fact that it was the last distillery to be built at Dufftown just before the turn of the century, that it can still be procured at the fortifying strength of 82.3 degrees of proof and at the perfect age of 12 years, and that it has found its way to many parts of the world from Japan to Mexico, remarkably little can be discovered about it.

First enquiries at Macdonald Greenlees, the agents in Edinburgh, will lead cross-country to the distillery at Dufftown. From there the intrepid explorer will be diverted to the head office of the Scottish Malt Distillers Company in Elgin. This is the malt whisky side of the Distillers Company which in turn owns Glendullan.

Having penetrated thus far our explorer will be little wiser and will probably leave with the impression that Glendullan is hardly ever sold except for export to exotic, far-flung places. This is not actually the case, as those whose eyes become accustomed to the enshrouding Celtic mist will discover. The occasional bottle can be found in its native Scotland.

Glenfarclas~Glenlivet

GLENFARCLAS, which is written in script
on the label, is believed to be a corruption of the
Gaelic 'Gleann-Fearann-Glas' which means 'Glen
of the Green Grassland.' Glenlivet itself is
derived from 'Glean-liobh-aite' meaning 'Glen of
the Smooth Place. There was even a much older
and now disused local place name, Dallasbrachti

Dallasbrachti 1262 A.D.

or Dolesbrachti as it was formerly spelt, from the
Celtic words meaning 'The Dale of the Malt House,'
which gave a hint that distilling might have been
carried on in this area from as long ago as 1262.

In 1836 a license for Glenfarclas Distillery
was taken out by one William Hay and in 1865 the
distillery was bought by J. and G. Grant, whose
successors still own and manage it.

The Grants came from Blairfindy Farm,
which is overlooked by the sixteenth century
remains of Blairfindy Castle. In the Jacobite
rebellion of 1745 two Grants of Blairfindy, David
and William, carried arms in Prince Charles's
army and afterwards 'submitted to the King's
mercy.'

Despite this period af adversity, the Grants prospered as farmers and J. and G. Grant at first looked upon Glenfarclas, which they had bought from Ballindalloch Estate, as an extension of their farming enterprises. For five years after 1865 they leased the distillery with all the equipment which they had bought from Hay's trustees to John Smith, the brewer from from Glenlivet. In 1870 Smith left to set up his own distillery and the Grants at last took up distilling themselves.

During the centenary of the Pot Malt Distillers Association in 1974 it fell to a Grant of Glenfarclas to be President of the association.

Glenfarclas welcomes visitors and has a specially designed reception centre which, besides an exhibition of the distillery's past, has a licence to sell a special bottling of its malt whisky at eight years old and 80 degrees of proof.

On loan from Customs and Excise is a is a confiscated illicit still — not, sadly, in working order. Small holes have, by regulation, been bored through the base.

Glenfarclas is a forceful Highland malt whisky, as every blender knows. It can be bought up to 15 years old and at a proof of up to 105 degrees.

Glenfiddich

GLENFIDDICH was the first pure single malt whisky to be nationally advertised. It can now be found throughout the UK, where it is one of the most popular malts. Abroad it is just as popular, with almost half the export malt whisky market.

This is the sister malt to Balvenie, which is just down the hill, although there are distinct differences of taste between them, for reasons which no one can quite explain.

William Grant of Glenfiddich was born in 1839, the son of a soldier who had served under Wellington in the Peninsular War. His first idea was to set up a lime works, but he lacked capital. In 1866 he went into Mortlach Distillery where he worked for 20 years. By 1887 he had saved up enough money to buy the equipment of the old Cardow distillery for £120.

With the help of his two eldest sons, one of whom later became a lawyer and the other a schoolmaster, he built Glenfiddich Distillery, and ran it with the help of his three younger sons. Two of the three younger boys became doctors, and the third bought Glendronach which is now part of Teacher's.

Old William Grant lived until 1923, when he died at the grand old age of 83.

Glenfiddich draws its water from the Robbie Dubh Spring, on the lower slopes of the Convals, two hills which dominate Dufftown. It is one of only two malt whiskies which are actually bottled at the distillery. At eight years of age it is put into those familiar triangular bottles and sold as Glenfiddich Pure Malt.

The original distillery buildings have been converted into a reception centre and museum for visitors, in excess of 50,000 being shown round each year by more than a dozen guides.

the first pure single malt whisky to be nationally advertised...

Glen Flagler

GLEN FLAGLER goes quite against the tradition that a single malt whisky should be named after the distillery from which it comes. It is distilled at Moffat Distillery in Airdrie and perhaps its makers are right in thinking that Moffat is not quite the name for a single malt whisky. All the same it takes a most vigorous scanning of the maps to find a Glen Flagler and there is a real risk of confusing this whisky with one of the many vatted (blended) malts.

The distillery is one of the most modern and it produces quite a pleasant and robust Lowland malt whisky. The water from which it is distilled comes from the quaintly named 'Lady Belle's Moss,'

no surviving
tradition as to
who Lady Belle......

although there is no surviving tradition as to why it was so called, or even who Lady Belle was.

Lately Glen Flagler has been promoted quite strongly in many parts of the world at five and eight years old and 70 degrees of proof. The older whisky comes in a glove of deep red, lettered in gold. Glen Flagler accepts, perhaps more readily than many single malt whiskies, a small admixture of water.

Glen Garioch

THE GLEN GARIOCH is one of the more recent of all malt whiskies to find its way into the bottle. Yet it comes from one of Scotland's oldest distilleries.

Only towards the end of 1972 did the management of Glengarioch Distillery decide to release in bottled form the very distinguished malt whisky which first originated there in 1797. (Just how long ago that was one can judge from the fact that, when the works were started, the local minister's stipend was £45 per annum plus half a chalder of victual and the local school-master's salary was £10 plus emoluments!)

Oldmeldrum is at the beginning of the valley of the Garioch, which stretches from there for twenty miles and forms the granary of Aberdeenshire. The area was for a long time dominated by the wild and unruly Comyns until King Robert the Bruce stormed their camp in 1307 and put their leader, the Earl of Buchan, to flight.

Barra Castle, only about a mile from the distillery, stands to the west of Barra Hill and very close to the site of this decisive victory. It is still the home of a family with very ancient connections in the neighbourhood.

Almost up to the turn of the century ox-wagons brought barley to the distillery doors and one 8 horse power steam engine drove all its machinery. Some things have changed but not the quality of the whisky itself, which still draws on the waters of pure local springs as well as that which runs down from Percock Hill on the beautiful estate of Meldrum House, now an hotel.

The Glen Garioch is described by its distillers as 'having a magnificently robust nose, flowery, not very smoky; it is surprisingly mild on the palate, and it is this quality which could well become the Glen Garioch signature. A crisp rather than bland finish, with a good firm aftertaste.'

Glengoyne

A NIP OF Glengoyne might be as good a start as any for those about to venture through the Trossachs into the Highlands. There should be no difficulty in getting it in Strathblane or the Black Bull in Killearn.

Glengoyne sits right on the Highland Line but since its waters are drawn from north of it, Glengoyne is classed as a Highland Malt Whisky.

The distillery was built in 1833, below a fine 50 foot waterfall at the foot of the Campsie Fells. Only about 200 yards from the distillery is the tree where Rob Roy was said to have hidden to evade his pursuers. And in later times Marshal of the RAF, Lord Tedder was born there, the son of the Excise Officer.

Rob Roy's Tree.

Shortly after the Second World War, when whisky was short and security momentarily lax, a little of the Rob Roy enterprise was revived by some intruders who tasted their way through the distillery, taking only the best.

Lang Brothers, who operate the distillery, were acquired by Robertson and Baxter Ltd. in 1965. The change brought a big modernisation programme and the opening, in 1968, of a new reception centre at the distillery. (For details of visiting times etc. see: 'Scotland's Distilleries: A Visitors' Guide').

At about the same time Lang's changed their label to a most striking and attractive design of two traditional pot stills on a black ground. This change has undoubtedly had a beneficial effect on sales of Glengoyne.

Glen Grant~Glenlivet

GLEN GRANT started in 1840, when the brothers John and James Grant moved their distillery from Dandaleith, where they'd been distilling whisky since 1834.

Legend has it that long before that they'd been whisky smugglers in Glenlivet. One of them had tried a spell as a solicitor in Elgin, but he found the law did not satisfy him, and he turned back, with profit, to distilling.

Some Glen Grant is matured in sherry casks and some in plain casks, the latter being clear of colour which gives it some curiousity value.

It is available in many degrees of maturity: 8, 15 years and even older, and it is best when really well matured. The distillery always puts the age on the whisky it bottles as well as the rather quaint Victorian label of two Highlanders around a barrel.

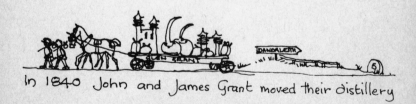

In 1840 John and James Grant moved their distillery

The Glenlivet

WHEN GEORGE SMITH of Glenlivet took out the first licence to set up a legal distillery in 1824 he had to contend with fierce opposition from the local smugglers. He carried in his belt a pair of hair-trigger pistols which had been presented to him by the laird of Aberlour.

Two distilleries which were started up in the next two years had to cease operations because of local opposition, and one was actually burned down.

In the end, Glenlivet became so famous that almost every distillery in the 'longest glen in Scotland' began to use the name. In 1880 recourse was made to law and Smith's Glenlivet became the only whisky entitled to call itself 'The Glenlivet'.

But it is hardly surprising Glenlivet should have become so popular. George IV insisted on Glenlivet, illicit at that time, whenever he came to the Highlands. In fact it was a timely gift in 1822 of 'Glenlivet whisky long in the wood, long in uncorked bottles, mild as milk and the true contraband gout in it', along with 50 brace of ptarmigan, that eventually secured the donor's father an Indian judgeship and made the family fortune.

thinks.....
must make
that man
an Indian
judge

George IV always
insisted on Glenlivet

When Smith, encouraged by the Duke of
Gordon, rebuilt his distillery at Upper Drumin, a
popular couplet went:
"Glenlivet has its castles three,
Drumin, Blairfindy and Deskie,
And also one distillery
More famous than the castles three."

And on the subject of rhymes, Macpherson
in W.E. Aytoun's poem 'had a son who married
Noah's daughter, and nearly spoiled ta flood, by
trinking up ta water: which he would have done

I at least believe it, had the mixture been only half Glenlivet.'

Professor Macdowall, a notable expert on Scottish pure malt whisky, says of Glenlivet that 'It has a deep mellowness and ripe fullness of flavour, together with a delicacy of aroma which is easy to recognize. It has a subtle peatiness without being aggressively peaty and gentle sweetness without any loss of freshness.'

The George Smith of Glenlivet anti-smuggler device.

Glen Mhor

INVERNESS has been making whisky since before the fourteenth century. Before 1775 it was the chief malting town in Scotland.

Glen Mhor distillery (Mhor is the Gaelic for great) was built in 1892 by the ex-provost, John Birnie J.P., in partnership with Mr James Mackinlay of Charles Mackinlay & Co. Ltd.

It was the first distillery in Scotland to introduce mechanical malting, but the distilling plant itself has remained unchanged, except that the stills are heated by steam instead of coal. And modernisation has in no way affected the character of Glen Mhor, which is very largely derived from the beautifully soft and peaty waters of Loch Ness.

Mr Neil Gunn, one of the greatest experts on malt whisky in Scotland, had a special affection for 'Glen Mhor', "Until a man has the luck to chance on a perfectly matured malt such as Glen Mhor, he does not really know what whisky is," he wrote.

Glen Mhor also owns a distillery of similar size and output only 100 yards away. Glen Albyn uses the same water, and almost identical equipment, yet both whiskies can be easily told apart.

There is a story that in the old days a pipe was laid from the spirit safe in Glen Albyn distillery to a public house nearby. The layer of the pipe was shipped to Australia, but returned a few years later and informed the Excise, so there, the story runs, was a pub that lost its licence and clients a ready source of refreshment! Unfortunately you cannot taste what they missed either, for Glen Albyn is not (at the time of writing at least) available on the UK market.

Glen Mhor can be bought at 10 years old and 75 degrees of proof, as well as at six years old and 70 degrees of proof.

Glen Mhor and Glen Albyn use the same water!

Glenmorangie

GLENMORANGIE is one of the most northern distilleries in Scotland. It looks across the Dornoch Firth with a distant view of the hills of Sutherland.

In the distillery grounds there is a large boulder, left by a retreating glacier of the ice age. It bears the rather unexpected inscription, 'The Immortal Walter Scott ob. 1832' which it is thought was chiselled by someone employed in the building of the distillery.

Although it is unusual to find a tribute to Sir Walter Scott so far north at that time, Glenmorangie formerly featured him, with dogs, on their labels. The picture was copied from the Princes Street monument, and surrounded by the words 'The Immortal Sir Walter Scott.'

Glenmorangie (morangie means haugh, or low level ground) is only a mile from the ancient town of Tain, granted its first charter by Malcolm Canmore.

From the eleventh century it had the right of sanctuary, which was violated continuously — as when in 1306 Robert the Bruce sent his children there and William, 4th Earl of Ross, promptly handed them over to the English.

From the 11th century Tain had the right of sanctuary.

In 1738 there was an important brewery there, and whisky distilling was carried on as an adjunct to farming at Morangie and Ardjackie farms. But in 1843 the brewery was converted into a distillery, which drew its water from two private springs in Tarlogie Hill.

Glenmorangie is a gentle and delicate whisky with some resemblance to a Lowland malt. It is bottled at 10 years old and 70 degrees of proof.

Glenrothes ~ Glenlivet

GLENROTHES distillery was built in 1878, a short way up the glen formed by the burn of Rothes which flows, brown, soft and clear from the Mannoch Hills.

It is described by one writer (Professor Daiches) as having "a strong peaty nose, if not the subtlest one of the fullest of Eastern Malts, a whisky of real character".

Which probably explains why another writer of the nineteenth century chose to append the following verses to Glenrothes:
"Gie him strong drink, until he wink,
That's sinking in despair;
An' liquor guid to fire his bluid,
That's prest wi' grief an care
Here let him bouze, an' deep carouse
Wi' bumpus flowing o'er,
'Til he forgets his loves or debts,
An' minds his griefs no more'.

William Cadenhead of Aberdeen bottled it at 10 years old and 80 degrees of proof. Matthew Gloag of Perth, who are the main agents for Glenrothes-Glenlivet, bottle it at eight years old but still have some at 20 years old.

Tradition is strong at Glenrothes, all the new stills being exact copies of the old ones.

Glen Scotia

GLEN SCOTIA is one of the last two distilleries in Campbeltown. Once upon a time, before the Crash in the 1920's, there were 32.

Glen Scotia is a rich, full, robust and peaty whisky with a slight suggestion of the oiliness of Irish whiskey — which is not altogether surprising when you consider the Irish coast is only 30 miles away.

FERGUS, first King of Scotland

The distillery was built in 1832 near the Parliament Square, where in 503 Fergus, the first king of Scotland, built his parliament house. It was from here until 843 that the affairs of Scotland were administered, and tradition has it that the Stone of Destiny upon which the sovereigns of Scotland were crowned came from this spot.

Subsequently the stone was moved from Scone by Edward I to Westminster Abbey.

The distillery was described in 1887 as "situated at the end of a subway and seems to have hidden itself away as if the making of whisky at the time was bound to be kept a dark secret."

For anyone who is not travelling locally, a bottle of Glen Scotia can still be procured from the proprietors of the distillery, A. Gillies & Co. Ltd., Newton Place, Glasgow.

"as if the making of whisky was bound to be kept a dark secret."

Glenturret

GLENTURRET is one of the oldest of Scotch malt whiskies. The distillery was established in 1775, and it is believed to have been originally in the hands of smugglers who selected the site for the special virtues of the Turret water. This beautiful spot is a little over two miles north east of one of the most painted glens in Scotland.

The Turret rises in Ben Chonzie, a mountain which is 3000 feet above sea level, where the snow lies until the end of June. It falls into the Turret Loch, and from there flows for about five miles to join the Earn.

It is not easy to come by Glenturret, except in its native haunts, where the sharp-eyed hunter should be watching out for a dram.

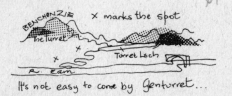

It's not easy to come by Glenturret...

Highland Park

HIGHLAND PARK is a very famous whisky from Kirkwall in the Orkneys, where there are no trees and the wind blows most of the time. At the higher degrees of proof it can be compared with the very finest of brandy but it can also be obtained at lower proof, around 75 degrees, from the Wine Society.

The site where the distillery now stands was where Magnus Eunson, the greatest and most accomplished of all the Orkney smugglers, had his bothy. By profession he was a church officer, but since he was also a distiller in private life, he kept a stock of whisky under the pulpit.

On one occasion, hearing that the church was to be searched for whisky by a party of excisemen, Eunson had the kegs removed to his house. They were placed in the middle of the room and covered with a clean white cloth. Under the cloth was a coffin lid, and as the excise officers approached, Eunson knelt with his bible, and the others with their psalm books. As the door door opened they set up a wail for the dead.

Eunson indicated there had been a death and one of the attendants whispered 'small-pox'. The excise officers evaporated.

The water supply comes from two wells, and traditionally a little heather has been used with every lot of peat to dry the malt. Some say they can taste the effect of this heather in Highland Park.

Highland Park — the Excisemen raid the house of Magnus Eunson.

Inchgower

INCHGOWER Highland malt whisky returned
to the market in 1972 after many years of absence.
It had been a popular whisky both in Great
Britain and the colonies as far back as the
late nineteenth century. For some reason it went
out of currency until its owners, Arthur Bell and
Sons Ltd., of Perth, made it available again.

In the last century a well-known smuggler
called Macpherson had his house on the high ground
opposite the distillery. His still, at the back of
the Bin Hill, was so well concealed that only when
some cattle strayed from the path and dislodged a
turf was the whole thriving enterprise revealed and
dismantled. The farmer claimed his reward, but
Macpherson and his collaborators escaped to sea
by boat.

The distillery was founded in 1871 and 25 years later a visitor was able to describe the space in front of the stills as 'sufficient to seat a small congregation to witness the progress of the work and spiritual mission carried on within its boundaries.'

Inchgower is bottled at 12 years old and 70 degrees of proof. It is mellow with a distinct hint of the peat over which its spring water passes.

Since whisky from this area has for generations fortified the fishermen of nearby Buckie, once the greatest herring fishing port in Britain, it might be considered a natural dram for those in peril, or just acute discomfort, on the sea.

Jura

ISLE OF JURA single malt whisky was to be available for public consumption during 1974.

The distillery, sited in a bay where a circlet of islands acts as a natural breakwater, is only a few yards from the cave which gave it its beginnings. As far back as 1502 illicit distilling had been carried on in this cave with such success that gradually all the other stills, from the Knochrome Headland right round the coast, began to gravitate towards this spot.

The burn which runs from the loch a thousand feet up in the hills actually passes through the cave and must have provided a ready supply of coolant for the emerging spirit.

The Isle of Jura Distillery was one of the very first to take out a licence. In 1880 it was largely re-built and re-equipped. It was the first distillery to be powered entirely by water turbines. In fact it was considered highly efficient by the standards of the time until it was observed that the 'spent wash' from the stills was pouring straight into a butt from which the local cattle were drinking — with remarkable results!

About 1900 the landlord of the distillery began to try to raise the rent. The tenant, a Mr Ferguson, upped and left with all his distilling equipment. So the landlord removed the roof to avoid paying rates and the buildings fell into a state of decay. For half a century after 1913 no whisky came out of Jura.

Then in 1957 two local landowners and a well-known distiller took stock of the grim drop in the island's population from a thousand souls in 1914 to a mere 150 some 40 years later. They decided to re-build the distillery and in 1963 the first spirit flowed from the new stills.

Jura is only a few minutes by ferry from Islay, but Isle of Jura malt whisky, bottled at eight years old and 70 degrees of proof, is entirely different from any Islay malt whisky. It stands on its own — gentle and light, but full-flavoured as a West Coast Highland malt whisky.

Some may detect in it characteristics that are reminiscent of Glenmorangie.

Knockando

KNOCKANDO is pronounced like the Gaelic words from which it is derived. 'Cnoc-an-Dhu' means the little black hillock.

Highland malt whisky has been made here on the Speyside since the turn of the century, but Knockando has only recently been marketed as a single malt whisky at 70 degrees of proof. The distillery is now owned by Justerini and Brooks. The whisky has already been well-received by the locals who may (dare one say it?) be an even more discriminating and critical panel than J. & B.'s customers at large.

Knockando has a traditional and austere bottle label which makes no concessions to popular advertising. It simply states the distillation season and bottling date to support the '12 year old' statement. This is important to those connoisseurs who hold that there are vintage seasons in malt whisky just as there are in wine.

1962 1963 1964 1965

there are vintage
seasons in malt whisky....

Lagavulin

LAGAVULIN is one of the oldest distilleries
in Islay. In a sense it was started in 1742 when
there were 10 small and separate smuggling
bothies for making 'moonlight' as opposed to the
'daylight'. Up to 1821 whole families in Islay
were supported entirely by smuggling, but
eventually they were absorbed into one
establishment which at first made only a few
thousand gallons of whisky a year.

The water for the whisky comes down over
moss and peat and innumerable small waterfalls
from the hill of Solan, where there are two lochs.
The distillery is built at the head of a small bay,
around which huge rocks like monsters rise from
the deep, producing weird effects when seen by
moonlight.

Nearby are the ruins of Dun-naomhaig Castle
which stands on a large promontory rock, protected
on the land side by a thick earthen mound opposite
the village of Lagavulin.

Lagavulin: huge rocks like monsters....

Laphroaig

LAPHROAIG has, perhaps, the strongest personality of any Scotch whisky. It has both devotees, who will drink nothing else, and detractors. It has been described as a "thick and pungent spirit of a peculiar peat reek flavour", and as having "a medicinal taste with a strong suggestion of iodine." It is perhaps the most strongly peated of all whiskies.

Despite this, Laphroaig has a unique and special charm when taken on appropriate occasions as with, for-instance, highly seasoned foods.

It has been distilled down by the sea shore not far from Port Ellen since 1820, bottled at 10 years old and 70 degrees of proof, Laphroaig became short not long ago as a bottled single malt whisky because of demand at home and abroad. Now at last the situation has returned to normal and this fine whisky is generally obtainable.

Laphroaig is now owned by Long John Distilleries Limited, who also produce the eight year old blend 'Islay Mist', which rates high among blends available and which, of course, makes use of Laphroaig.

Linkwood

LINKWOOD is the single malt whisky of a
very charming small distillery which you'll find
in a wood near Elgin. It was built in 1821 and
named after an old mansion house that formerly
stood on the site.

Linkwood owes a lot of its reputation to a
Mr Roderick Mackenzie who came from Wester
Ross and for many years supervised the distilling.
If he could avoid it he never replaced a single
item of equipment, or it was said, allowed a
spider's web to be removed, lest any variation
from tradition should affect the character of the
whisky. This caution is common among distillers
but Mr Mackenzie carried it to a high degree.

an old mansion house that formerly
stood on the site.....

Professor Macdowall has said of Linkwood
that it is a "pleasant light whisky with a typical
Glenlivet flavour, although it reminds me of a
lowland Rosebank." It is not a well-known whisky
but has long been classified as one of the best.

It is generally available in bottle at 12
years old and at 70 and 75 degrees of proof.

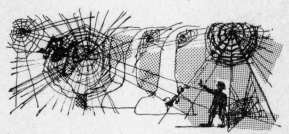

Mr Roderick Mackenzie never allowed a spider's
web to be removed

Littlemill

THE DATE WHEN whisky was first distilled
at Littlemill will probably never be known.
Perhaps it was in the fourteenth century when the
Colquohouns built Dunglas Castle to control the
ford across the Clyde, and to act as a bastion to
the more important castle at Dumbarton.

What is known is that in about 1750 George
Buchanan, a wealthy maltster in Glasgow, bought
Littlemill as part of the Auchterlonie estate, and
that in 1772, houses were built for excise officers.

By 1821, when the first Government survey
of the industry was made, Littlemill was making
20,000 gallons of whisky a year.

Although most of the production of the
distillery, which is now owned by Barton
Distilling (Scotland) Ltd., goes towards blending
their House of Stuart whisky, it is featured as a
pure single malt at 75 degrees proof in the lists
of a few specialist stockists.

Longmorn~Glenlivet

LONGMORN-GLENLIVET is a connoisseur's Highland malt whisky. The name is probably derived from the Welsh word Lhangmorgund, morgund meaning a holy man. The distillery warehouse now stands on the site of what, it is thought, was once a chapel.

The water for Longmorn comes from a local spring which never dries and the peat is obtained from nearby Mannoch Hill.

Longmorn single malt whisky can be obtained at eight years old and 70 degrees of proof. It is famous for its terrific bouquet, which can stand comparison with that of a glass of the finest after dinner brandy.

Professor Daiches records having drunk it at 68 years old from a newly broached cask. Although naturally a little thin, it was still apparently "mellow and pleasant."

Longmorn is probably derived from the Welsh word for holy man.

12 yr old
very mellow
18 yr old smooth!

Macallan

THE FACT THAT Macallan was one of the first to take out a licence in 1824 suggests that whisky had been distilled on Macallan Farm long before that, probably for the uplift of cattle drovers. For throughout the eighteenth century cattle from the Highlands were driven down to such Lowland markets as Falkirk, and one of the few fords over the Spey was at Macallan, just below the distillery. The stances which held the cattle are still distinguishable.

Macallan whisky was brewed for the uplift of the drovers.

The distillery has been in the Kemp family since 1892. Roderick Kemp, the first owner, had previously owned and managed Talisker Distillery on the Isle of Skye and he brought his great experience to bear on Macallan, which continued to expand steadily throughout the bad years of the First World War and the Depression.

For six years from 1950 the distillery was expanded in such a way as not to disturb production. Further modifications in 1959 still failed to increase the capacity enough, so that a second distillery had to be built between 1964 and 1966 to double output.

The Macal'an, which is rich and smooth in flavour, ranks very high among all the Scotch single malt whiskies. During the 1956 visit of Kruschev and Bulganin, Macallan was chosen to be offered as an alternative to cognac at the Mansion House dinner in their honour.

Kruschev and Bulganin drank Macallan in 1956.

Miltonduff~Glenlivet

MILTONDUFF is distilled in the barley
rich plain of Pluscarden, the 'Garden of Scotland.'
At the head of the vale in a secluded and
beautifully wooded glen, stand the ruins of
Pluscarden Priory. This ancient monastic
establishment, founded in 1230 by Alexander II,
was said to have been one of the richest in
Scotland. The Miltonduff Distillery now occupies
part of the site.

The Benedictine monks of Pluscarden were
said to have been experts in the art of brewing
fine ales, the quality of which was among the
best in Scotland. It "made the hearts of all
rejoice, and filled the abbey with unutterable
bliss, raised their devotions to that pitch that
Heldon's Hills echoed their hallelujahs."

Milton-Duff filled the Abbey with unutterable bliss.........

The monks brewed their ales from the Black
Burn, which descends from the mossy uplands of

the Black Hills and runs through the plain. An ancient abbot, accompanied by priors, palmers and priests, invoked a blessing on the waters and from that time the drink distilled from them was christened 'aqua vitae', water of life.

The stone on which the abbot knelt was said to have been built into the malt mill, and the old mash house of the distillery which was rebuilt in 1824, was once the brewhouse of the monks.

Miltonduff which is now owned by Hiram Walker is bottled at 13 years of age and 85 degrees of proof.

an ancient abbot, accompanied
by priors, palmers and priests...

Mortlach-Glenlivet

MORTLACH DISTILLERY lies in the hollow where in 1010 the Danes were defeated by Malcolm II, second king of Scotland.

The Danes had been attracted by the pleasant bowl and camped in it — the word Mortlach means bowl shaped valley. King Malcolm had however taken the precaution of damming the river Dullan, a mile or so upstream and during the night he broke the dam. The unsuspecting Danes were overwhelmed by the flood of water and Scots.

Mortlach means a bowl shaped valley which attracted the Danes as a camping site.

To show his gratitude, Malcolm added three spears' lengths to Mortlach church which had been founded in 556 AD.

The distillery itself was built in 1823, and draws its water from the Conval Hills and the famous Priest's Well. It is of very fine quality. The whisky it makes is full and fruity, but with little of the taste of peat.

Oban

OBAN is distilled from the waters which flow from two lochs in Ardconnel, a mile above Oban

It is an old distillery which was built in 1794 by the Stephenson family who founded Oban as a centre of Highland industry and commerce. Until the Stephensons, Oban was just another fishing village.

Oban single malt does not fall into any of the usual classifications — Islay, Campbeltown, Speyside or Lowland Malt. It is therefore particularly interesting to taste it against the others.

Old Fettercairn

FETTERCAIRN has a few other claims to fame apart from its local malt. It was here in AD 994 that Finella is said to have done King Kenneth III to death by means of a crossbow device activated by a golden apple.

It was also here, in 1864, that a Royal Arch was built to commemorate an incognito visit of Queen Victoria and Prince Albert.

But long before 1824, when the present distillery was built, Fettercairn was a headquarters of smuggling. Higher up the mountains, on the slopes of Cairn — o' — Mount, in the Grampians, an illicit still was in operation. There was always very superior water from the Grampians to be drawn on.

Old Fettercairn, bottled at five years old, is called 575 to denote its age and strength, similarly 875 denotes 8 year old whisky.

(Old Fettercairn)

10 yr
Dark color
Strong taste slightly
sweet light on tongue
w/tickle in back of
throat after
swallowing

Old Pulteney

OLD PULTENEY is the most northerly of all the mainland malt whiskies and, as one of the experts has put it, "it has some of the strong characteristics of the northern temperament. It has to be treated with respect."

The distillery stands in a wind-battered, sea-pounded area with ancient ruined castles all around. Auldwich Castle, the Auld Man of Wick, is close by. It is a most unlikely area for a distillery except for the ease of communication by sea and the presence of the splendid peaty waters of the Loch of Hempriggs.

The distillery was closed down during the bad times in 1926, and only re-opened in 1951. Now owned by Hiram Walker it is once again in full production.

Old Pulteney has a peatiness that is subtle and not too strong. It is a whisky with a fine bouquet, and one of the fastest maturing of all Scotch whiskies.

..has to be treated with respect....

Ord

ORD malt whisky is distilled from the magnificent water which comes from Glen Oran and from two lochs in the hills of Knockudas. The Oran burn passes close to the roofs of some of the buildings.

Glen Oran was a favourite resort of smugglers right up to the end of the nineteenth century when secret stills were still being discovered. The site of the distillery itself was a smugglers' bothy early in the century, but it was not until 1838 that it was turned into a legal distillery.

There are two standing stones in the Muir of Ord which commemorate an ancient feat of arms connected with the prophesied extinction of the clan Mackenzie. Despite this, however the Mackenzies provided not long ago a proprietor for the distillery and they still constitute a fair proportion of the local consumers.

As with Highland Park, heather is traditionally mixed with peat in the drying of the malt.

Heather is traditionally mixed with peat

Rosebank

ROSEBANK might seem something of a misnomer when you see the industrial setting of the distillery. But the whisky is very excellent and lightly flavoured — and very definitely a Lowland malt. It is a specially good introduction to malt whisky for those who find the character of other malts a little too forceful.

Distilling has been carried on there since 1798 — the site chosen no doubt for its inexhaustible supply of water. In 1864 the distillery was reconditioned.

Springbank

ONLY THE FINEST of the Campbeltown distilleries survived the bad years of the 1920's; two in fact out of what had once been 32. In the heyday of Campbeltown's distilling it was said that a skipper could find his way into harbour in a thick fog by the bouquet of the stills.

Springbank — a skipper finds his way into harbour with the help of his nose....

It is thought that whisky and the art of making it was brought to the Campbeltown area of Kintyre by the Celts from Antrim before the end of the sixth century and that it was later spread to other areas of Scotland.

Springbank Distillery is almost unique among Scottish distilleries in that it is still owned by descendants of its founders, the Mitchells, Scotland's oldest distilling family. The present distillery was built in 1828 on the site of the previous illicit distillery of Archibald Mitchell, the great great grandfather of the present managing director.

In Springbank the 'foreshots' and 'feints' which are the impure spirit from the beginning and end of each distillation, are re-distilled in a separate still instead of going back into the low wines still for re-distillation, which is what usually happens elsewhere.

This may account for Springbank's special kind of mellowness and lightness and such epithets as rich, yet not heavy, soft, fragrant, smooth, gentle, well-finished etc. being used to describe it.

The Celts brought whisky to Campbeltown from Co. Antrim.

Springbank's own description of its whisky is rather charming and unusual: "The fullness of flavour and absence of fire should be noticed. Notice also the even centre of the palate taste. This may be contrasted with the greatest of Islay whiskies which are concentrated on the back of the tongue and with those of the finest Highland (Speyside) malts, which seem to be split into two parts, one forward in the mouth and one at the rear."

Only limited quantities are available at 12 years old and 80 degrees of proof. Along with Glenfiddich it is the only single malt whisky to be bottled at the distillery itself. For the true enthusiast there are occasional bottles of 50 year old Springbank. It is also available to varying degrees of proof.

Strathisla ~ Glenlivet

Strathisla: where a battle was fought

STRATHISLA comes from Keith, where a great battle was fought in the old church yard by the banks of the river Isla. In 1646 the Duke of Montrose emerged as victor, but five years later he was to appear on the same banks as a captive; betrayed by a former adherent McLeod of Assynt.

Later in 1667 Peter Roy Macgregor, a predecessor of Rob Roy, who was then aged nine, invaded the town and attempted to hold it to ransom. But the townspeople of Strathisla, led by their local lairds, managed to beat him off. Shortly afterwards he was caught and executed.

The distillery is an old one, dating from 1786 and still, under the management of Chivas Bros, preserving its former charm.

The water for Strathisla whisky comes from
a spring which rises in the hills above the distillery.
It is collected in a reservoir which is said to be
haunted nightly by the fays and fairies.

The flavour has been described as "full and
fragrant, somewhere between Glenlivet and
Mortlach."

Peter Roy Macgregor
in 1667

Talisker

TALISKER is the only whisky distilled in the island of Skye. It is named after a nearby farm, but the distillery actually stands in the village of Carbost, drawing its water from the Carbost burn. The burn runs down the slope of Stockveil hill, a gentle slope of six or seven hundred feet to the shore of Loch Harport from which the distillery is supplied with malt by steamer.

The distillery was begun in 1843 and is well worth a visit as much for its fine views of the Cuillin Hills as anything else.

In 1916, Talisker distillery was taken over by the Distillers Company and there has been some criticism in recent times that, although it has retained its subtlety of flavour, it is not as

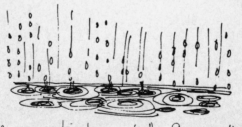

the uncertainties of the Skye weather.

mellow as it once was. It is a light whisky with a peaty flavour, but not so strongly peated as the Islay malts. It can be bought at the usual strengths of 70 and 80—as well as 100 degrees of proof.

Mr Neil Gunn, a noted connoisseur, has said of Talisker, 'At its best it can be superb, but I have known it to adopt the uncertainties of the Skye weather.'

Tamdhu~Glenlivet

TAMDHU Distillery stands right on the banks of the river Spey. It was built in 1897 and now it is in the hands of Highland Distilleries.

So enthusiastically has it been received abroad that as a matter of policy it is not being promoted in the UK. Some can still be found in the bottle, and it is well worth tasting before it becomes too much of a rarity.

Tamnavulin~Glenlivet

THERE IS a commonly held belief that great malt whisky can come only from old distilleries. In the early days of distilling the waters of Scotland were thoroughly tested by innumerable illicit stills which were themselves capable of infinite modification and experiment. So that in the end those that were not so good among them tended to give way to their betters. And when they came to build the great legal distilleries of our time they took the trouble to put them on what had been proved to be the most propitious sites.

Tamnavulin means 'The mill on the hill' and the new distillery was built near an ancient mill on the banks of the Livet itself. The designers of its stills were able to draw on long experience to adapt them to the local waters.

Tamnavulin means 'the Mill on the Hill'

According to locality every still differs in design, both at the point of boiling the liquor and in the 'stretching' and control of the rising vapour so that such particular elements as are not required in the final spirit fall away. There is no question of there being a standard pot to suit all waters.

Tamnavulin was tested for several years and today it would seem that this single malt whisky, with its label which uses the old Celtic form of lettering, can stand comparison with the older glenlivets. It is available in bottle at 75 degrees of proof.

Tomatin

TOMATIN single malt whisky comes from the largest malt distillery of all with an annual capacity of 5,000,000 gallons of malt whisky. It is owned by an independent company, quoted on the London stock exchange, the only single malt distillery with this distinction.

It was based on a small fifteenth century distillery which supplied the needs of men attending the local market before they and their animals began the long trek south through the hills.

It is a light-bodied and peaty flavoured malt, not unlike Glenlivet, but with a more emphatic taste of peat.

Tomatin : a small 15th century distillery supplying the needs of men on their way to market.

Tomintoul-Glenlivet

TOMINTOUL-GLENLIVET began to appear in bottles at the end of 1972. It is the third Highland malt distillery to be opened in Scotland since the war, and the first to be built and financed by Scottish capital in the Speyside this century.

The water is obtained from the Ballantuan spring only five hundred yards from the distillery, and observations were kept up on it for a year before the decision on the site was made final. Work on the distillery began in November 1964 and went on right through the winter at temperatures often as much as five or ten degrees below zero until equipment began to arrive the following March.

Tomintoul is the highest distillery in Scotland, being over 1100 feet above sea level. The village is a mecca for climbers and travellers in the Avon valley and along the Lecht road. A little fortification with T-G might not be ill-advised, though you may not find it easy to adjust to such a drastic departure from traditional bottle design.

Tormore

TORMORE comes from what has been called the Golden Rectangle in the heart of the Speyside country.

It was the first completely new malt distillery to be built this century in the Highlands of Scotland. Building began in the spring of 1958, and the distillery was opened in October 1960. It was designed by Sir Albert Richardson K.C.V.O. a past President of the Royal Academy, and is worth a visit as an elegant and striking contribution to modern industrial architecture.

Tormore is bottled at 10 years old and 70 degrees of proof. It is a typical Speyside malt which, although marketed for only a comparatively short time, has already won high commendation from whisky connoisseurs. Like Laphroaig, it is owned by Long John International Ltd.

Tullibardine

TULLIBARDINE is at Blackford in Perthshire, a small town which derives its name from the ancient tradition that the 'Fair Queen' Helen of Scotland was drowned at this spot some time before the Norman invasion of Britain.

But there are also happier associations with these waters. They were used by an ancient brewery which occupied the site of the present distillery. In fact it was with water from these same Ochil Hills that ale was brewed for James IV when he passed through Blackford after his coronation at Scone in 1488. We are told that the new king drank it with approval.

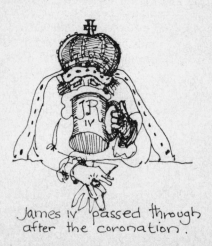

James IV passed through after the coronation.

We even have some idea of what this ale, or porter as it was later called, was probably like. A former owner of Tullibardine Distillery found a bottle so well sealed that it was still full flavoured and drinkable — with something of the colour of tawny port.

It is a short step from brewing to distilling, the making of beer being, as it were, the first part of the distilling process. So it was not difficult to convert the old brewery into a distillery.

The distillery takes its name from the nearby Tullibardine Moor on which the mighty Gleneagles Hotel now stands. A measure of Tullibardine pure malt consumed after lunch should carry golfers serenely down the first few fairways of the afternoon.

Further Details

MANY of the distilleries mentioned in this guide are represented by agents in Edinburgh and Glasgow. They, rather than the distilleries themselves, should be approached for further details about any particular whisky. In cases of difficulty the publishers will endeavour to forward enquiries to the appropriate source.

ABERLOUR-GLENLIVET
White Heather Distillers Ltd
127 St Vincent St., Glasgow G2

ARDBEG
Ardbeg Distillery Ltd
121 St Vincent St., Glasgow G2

AUCHENTOSHAN
Eadie Cairns Ltd
12 Waterloo Street, Glasgow G2

AULTMORE
John & Robert Harvey Ltd
75 Hope Street, Glasgow G2

BALBLAIR/OLD PULTENEY/
MILTONDUFF-GLENLIVET
Hiram Walker & Sons Ltd
Dumbarton G82

BALVENIE/GLENFIDDICH
William Grant & Sons Ltd
208 W. George St., Glasgow G2

BLADNOCH
Bladnoch Distillery Ltd
143 W. George St., Glasgow

BLAIR ATHOL/INCHGOWER
DUFFTOWN-GLENLIVET
Arthur Bell & Sons Ltd
Perth Scotland

BOWMORE/GLEN GARIOCH
Stanley Morrison (Agencies) Ltd
13 Royal Crescent, Glasgow G3

BRUICHLADDICH/DEANSTON MILL/
TULLIBARDINE/TAMNAVULIN-GVT
The Invergordon Distillers Ltd
181 W. George Street, Glasgow G2

CAPERDONICH/LONGMORN-GVT/
GLEN GRANT/GLENLIVET
The Glenlivet Distillers Ltd
45 Frederick Street, Edinburgh

CARDHU
John Walker and Sons Ltd
Kilmarnock KA3 1HD

CLYENLISH
Ainslie and Heilbron (Dist.) Ltd
5 Oswald Street. Glasgow C1

DALMORE
Dalmore, Whyte & Mackay Ltd
302/4 St Vincent Street, Glasgow G2

DEANSTON MILL (see Bruichladdich)

DUFFTOWN-GLENLIVET (see Blair
(see Blair Athol)

GLENDEVERON
William Lawson Distillers Ltd
288 Main Street, Coatbridge

GLENDRONACH
William Teacher & Sons Ltd
St. Enoch's Square, Glasgow

GLENFARCLAS-GLENLIVET
J. & G. Grant

Glenfarclas-Glenlivet Distillery
Ballindalloch, Banffshire

GLENFIDDICH (see Balvenie)

GLEN FLAGLER
Inver House Distillers Ltd
143 W. George St., Glasgow G1

GLEN GARIOCH (see Bowmore)

GLENGOYNE
Lang Bros. Ltd.
Dumgogyne, Stirlingshire

GLEN GRANT GLENLIVET/
GLENLIVET (see Caperdonich)

GLEN MHOR

Scottish Malt Distillers Ltd
Elgin

GLENMORANGIE
MacDonald & Muir Ltd
Queen's Dock, Leith

GLENROTHES-GLENLIVET
Matthew Gloag & Son Ltd
Bordeaux House, Perth

GLEN SCOTIA
A. Gillies & Co. Ltd
4 Newton Place, Glasgow G3 7PE

GLENTURRET
Glenturret Distillery
Crieff, Perthshire

HIGHLAND PARK/MACALLAN/
TAMDHU-GLENLIVET
Robertson & Baxter Ltd
106 W. Nile Street, Glasgow

INCHGOWER (see Blair Athol)

JURA
Isle of Jura Distillery,
Isle of Jura, Argyll

KNOCKANDO
Justerini & Brooks Ltd
39 George Street
Edinburgh EH2

LAGAVULIN
White Horse Distillers Ltd
Borron Street, Glasgow G4 9XF

LAPHROAIG/TORMORE
Long John Distilleries Ltd
55 Blythswood Street, Glasgow C2

LINKWOOD
John McEwan & Co. Ltd
Leith

LITTLEMILL
Barton Distilling (Scotland) Ltd
Alexandria, Dumbartonshire

LONGMORN-GLENLIVET
(see Caperdonich)

MACALLAN (see Highland Park)

MILTONDUFF-GLENLIVET
(see Balblair)

MORTLACH-GLENLIVET
Mortlach Distillery
Dufftown, Banffshire

OBAN
Scottish Malt Distillers Ltd
Elgin

OLD FETTERCAIRN
Fettercairn Distillery
Fettercairn, Kincardineshire

OLD PULTENEY (see Balblair)

ORD
Peter Dawson Ltd
75 Hope Street, Glasgow C2

ROSEBANK
Distillers Agency Ltd
65 Pall Mall, London SW1

SPRINGBANK
J. & A. Mitchell,
Springbank Dist.
Campbeltown, Argyllshire

STRATHISLA-GLENLIVET
Chivas Bros. Ltd
111 Renfrew Road, Paisley,

TALISKER
Dailuain-Talisker Distilleries Co.
1 Trinity Road, Elgin, Morayshire.

TAMDHU-GLENLIVET
(see Highland Park)

TAMNAVULIN (see Bruichladdich)

TOMATIN
Tomatin Distillers Co. Ltd
34 Dover Street, London W1

TOMINTOUL-GLENLIVET
Tomintoul-Glenlivet Distillery Co
302 St Vincent St., Glasgow G2

TORMORE (see Laphroaig)

TULLIBARDINE (see Bruichladdich)

THE MALT DISTILLERS' ASSOCIATION
OF SCOTLAND
(Formerly The Pot Still Malt Distillers'
Association of Scotland)
1 North Street
Elgin, IV30 1VA

THE SCOTCH WHISKY ASSOCIATION
20 Atholl Crescent
Edinburgh
031 - 229 4383

17 Half Moon Street
London W1
01 - 629 4384

ACADEMY OF PURE MALT WHISKY
c/o William Grant & Sons Ltd
40 Piccadilly
London W1V 9PA
01 - 734 2316

C. MUIRHEAD & SON
63 George Street
Edinburgh EH2
031 - 225 5736

GORDON & MACPHAIL
South Street
Elgin IV30
Elgin 2662

LAMBERT BROS.
9 Frederick Street
EDINBURGH EH2

P & J CAMPBELL
Tomintoul
Ballindalloch
Banffshire

STRACHAN of
Royal Deeside
Aboyne, Aberdeenshire

JOHN MILROY Ltd
3 Greek Street
London W1V 5LA

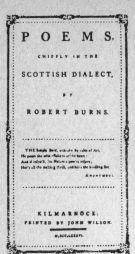

The Kilmarnock Edition of Robert Burns's poems, published in 1786, is now a very rare book.

This Kilmarnock facsimile has been printed on the finest mould made rag paper and is presented in a full leather binding, with the pages left uncut.

Just one thousand numbered copies are being produced in a limited edition that will appeal to lovers of poetry and fine books throughout the world.

Famedram Publishers Gartocharn Alexandria Dunbartonshire Scotland UK
Phone: Gartocharn 340
Telex: 77572 Gartan G

Reprinted in a Limited Edition

The Kilmarnock BURNS

Numbered Copies Bound in Real Leather

Read the
Small Print

Famedram guides
are
Written
Printed and
Published

in Scotland